W9-CDZ-620

BUTTERFLIES, BUGS, AND WORMS

SALLY MORGAN

Kingfisher

NEW YORK

KINGFISHER
Larousse Kingfisher Chambers Inc.
95 Madison Avenue
New York, New York 10016

First edition 1996

(HC) 10 9 8 7 6 5 4 3 2 1
(PB) 10 9 8 7 6 5 4 3 2 1

LIBRARY OF CONGRESS CATALOGING-IN-
PUBLICATION DATA
Morgan, Sally.
  Butterflies, bugs, and worms / Sally
Morgan.—1st ed.
    p.   cm.—(Young Discoverers)
  Includes index.
  Summary: Provides basic information about
the structure and habits
of a host of minibeasts, accompanied by a
variety of experiments.
1. Invertebrates—Juvenile literature. [1.
Invertebrates.
2. Invertebrates—Experiments. 3.
Experiments.] I. Title.
II. Series.
QL362.4.M 68   1996
595—dc20 96-963 CIP AC

ISBN 0-7534-5037-2 (HC)
ISBN 0-7534-5036-4 (PB)

Editor: Molly Perham **Designer:** Ben
White **Art editor:** Val Wright
Consultant: Michael Chinery **Photo
research:** Elaine Willis **Cover design:**
John Jamieson **Illustrations:** Peter Bull p.
4 (top right), 7, 10 (bot.), 13 (bot.), 15
(top), 18 (bot. left), 21 (bot.), 23, 26, 28,
29; Richard Draper p. 10 (top), 11, 14-15,
15 (center & bot.); Angelica Elsebach p.
20, 21 (top); Nick Hall p. 8 (top & left),
12, 13 (top), 14 (left), 18 (left), 23 (bot.);
Ruth Lindsay p. 22 (top), 30; Adam
Marshall p. 18-19; Chris Orr p. 6, 8-9, 9
(right); Michelle Ross p. 17 (bot.), 27;
Joyce Tuhill p. 16-17; Phil Weare p. 31;
Wendy Webb p. 4-5 **Photographs:** BBC
Natural History Unit p. 10 (Niall Benvie);
Bruce Colemanp. 5, 6, 24, 28 (Jane
Burton), 13(J. Brackenbury), 18 (Jeff Foott);
Michael Chinery p. 19; Ecoscene p. 30
(Alexandra Jones); NHPA p. 17 (Stephen
Dalton), 21 (R. & D. Keller), 23 (Anthony
Bannister)

Printed in Spain

About This Book

Not just about butterflies, bugs, and worms, this book also looks at where snails, spiders, and insects live, what they eat, how they move, and how they defend themselves. It also suggests lots of experiments and things to look for.

You should be able to find nearly everything you need for the experiments in your home, or in a garden, park, or nearby woodland. Walkingsticks can be found outside or bought in pet stores. Always put wild creatures back where you found them when you finish an experiment.

Activity Hints

• Before you begin an experiment, read through the instructions carefully and collect all the things you need.

• When you have finished, put everything away and wash your hands.

• Start a special notebook so that you can keep a record of what you do.

Contents

What is It?

Because there are so many kinds of animals, zoologists begin by dividing them into two groups: animals with a backbone (vertebrates) and animals without a backbone (invertebrates). There are many other names that are used to identify groups of small invertebrates. Arthropods, the largest group, include insects, crustaceans, millipedes, centipedes, and spiders. Cnidaria are soft, water-living creatures, including sea anemones and jellyfish. Worms are also invertebrates; so are mollusks, a group that includes snails and slugs.

To make it easier, some people refer to all of these small, spineless creatures as "minibeasts."

Caught in Amber

Millions of years ago, some insects were caught in sticky resin that oozed from the bark of pine trees. When this hardened and became amber, the insects were preserved inside.

Minibeasts vary in size, shape, and color. Scorpions and spiders have eight legs, while butterflies, bees, and fleas have six, and earthworms and sea anemones have no legs at all. The starfish has a spiny covering, and the snail has a coiled shell that protects its soft body.

No Backbone

A fish has a backbone, a bony rod running the length of its body. A crab has no backbone. Instead, it has a heavy, protective outer covering.

earthworm

sea anemone

butterfly

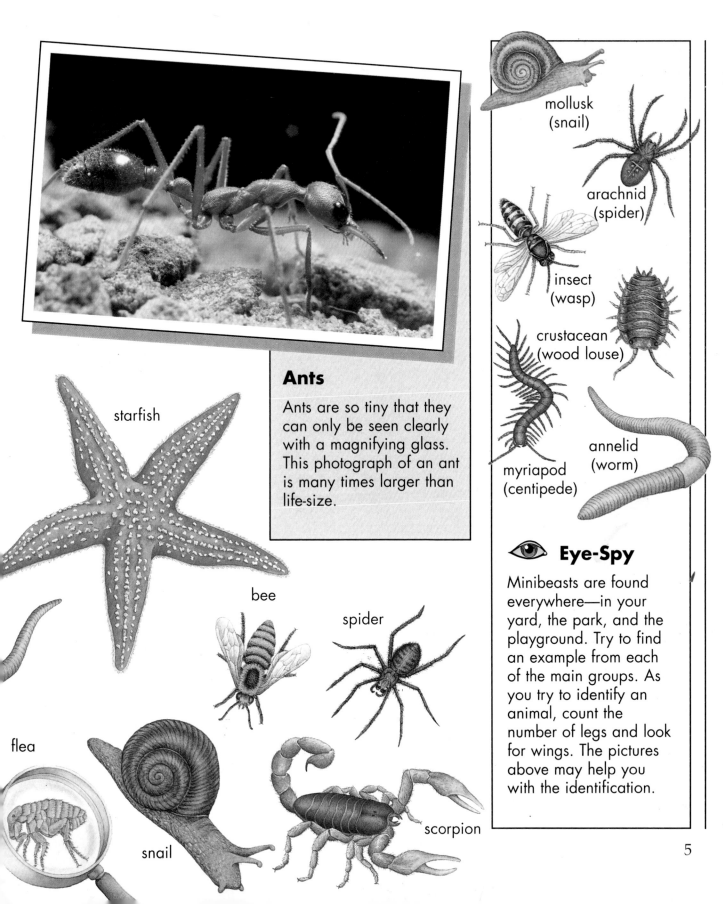

mollusk
(snail)

arachnid
(spider)

insect
(wasp)

crustacean
(wood louse)

myriapod
(centipede)

annelid
(worm)

Ants

Ants are so tiny that they can only be seen clearly with a magnifying glass. This photograph of an ant is many times larger than life-size.

starfish

bee

spider

flea

snail

scorpion

👁 Eye-Spy

Minibeasts are found everywhere—in your yard, the park, and the playground. Try to find an example from each of the main groups. As you try to identify an animal, count the number of legs and look for wings. The pictures above may help you with the identification.

Growing Up

Caterpillars and butterflies look very different, but they are actually the same animal at different stages in life. The caterpillar, in the growing stage, eats plants. Once it is fully grown, it enters the pupal stage. This is when the body of the caterpillar is completely reorganized into the body of a butterfly. After a few weeks, the case of the pupa splits open and the adult emerges. This complete change in appearance is called metamorphosis.

Courtship

The male fiddler crab attracts a female by waving his large claw. Different waves have different meanings.

The female butterfly lays her eggs on leaves. The eggs hatch within a few days and the young caterpillars feed on the leaves, growing rapidly. After a few weeks they pupate and undergo their metamorphosis.

1. egg

2. caterpillar

3. pupa

5. adult

4. new adult

Do it yourself

Walkingsticks are easy to keep as pets.

1. You will need a large plastic container, such as an old aquarium, with a lid.

2. Walkingsticks feed on privet and blackberry leaves, so collect some for food. Keep the plants fresh by wrapping tissue paper around the bottom of the stems, and putting them in a small plastic container of water.

3. Put in another small container of water, for drinking.

4. The walkingsticks may start to lay eggs. The eggs are tiny, round, and brown, and are easily confused with droppings. Collect the eggs and keep them in a small container until they hatch.

Locust Life Cycle

A locust egg hatches into a small hopper. It looks like an adult, but it is much smaller and lacks wings. The hopper grows rapidly, eating its own body weight in leaves each day. Every few days, it molts its skin to grow larger. At the fifth and final molt, the adult locust appears, complete with a set of wings.

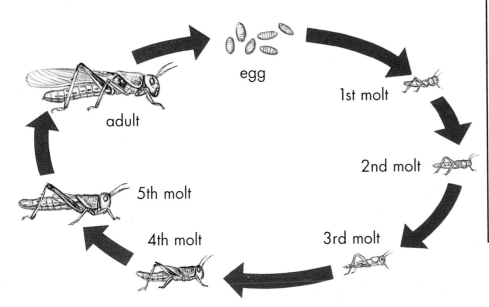

adult
egg
1st molt
2nd molt
3rd molt
4th molt
5th molt

👁 Eye-Spy

Female butterflies lay their eggs on the leaves of plants that the caterpillars like to eat. Nettles are popular, and you may find several types of caterpillars feeding on them. Look for caterpillars and make a note of the plants you find them on.

7

Plant Eaters

Plants are an important source of food for many minibeasts. Animals that eat only plants are called herbivores. Most herbivores eat a wide range of plant food, especially leaves, but some feed on just fruit, pollen, or nectar. Herbivores are the first link in the food chain because they feed on plants. They, in turn, are eaten by larger animals called carnivores, the meat eaters.

Honey Ants

Honey ants store nectar and honeydew in their bodies until they become too fat to move.

Do it yourself

See how many minibeasts you can find in the leaves of a tree.

1. Place a large white sheet under a low branch.

2. Give the branch a good shake. All the minibeasts living on that branch will fall onto your sheet.

3. Examine the animals you have caught. Those with wings will probably fly away, but the others will remain. Some of the more common minibeasts you might find are crab and wolf spiders, lacewings, green caterpillars, fruit flies, gall wasps, and weevils. There may also be several different types of beetles.

Plant eaters can be found wherever there are plants. Some plant eaters feed on leaves, and others suck nectar from flowers. A few can pierce plant stems to suck out sap, which is full of sugar.

hummingbird hawkmoth

crane fly

bee

bluebottle fly

shield bug

slug

ladybug

earwig

aphids

grasshopper

spider

👁 Eye-Spy

Look out for signs of plant eaters in your yard or school grounds—nibbled leaves, white marks produced by leaf miners, and oak galls, swellings where tiny wasps have laid their eggs.

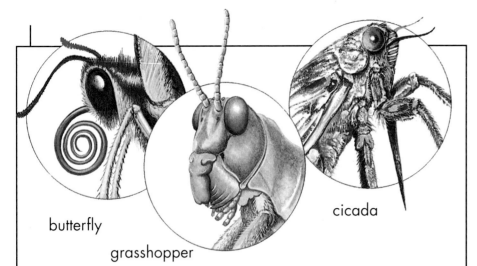

butterfly

grasshopper

cicada

Mouthparts for Different Foods

The mouthparts of insects are suited to their particular type of food. Butterflies uncoil a long thin proboscis to reach into flowers and suck out the nectar. Grasshoppers have strong biting jaws. Cicadas have piercing mouthparts that are used to suck sap from the plant stem.

Grazing Limpets

Limpets have a rough tongue called a radula, which they use to scrape algae off rocks.

Do it yourself

At night, moths are attracted to bright lights.

1. On a summer night, hang a white sheet on a clothesline.

2. Shine a strong flashlight through the sheet and watch the moths flying around in silhouette on the other side.

How It Works

Many moths fly at night in search of food. They are distracted by bright lights and come spiraling into them.

Hunters and Trappers

Many minibeasts feed on other animals. These are meat eaters—the carnivores. They are very powerful for their size and are ferocious hunters. Carnivores can move fast and have good eyesight so that they can spot their prey moving among leaves or flying through the air.

Hunters and trappers can be found in hidden places of the woodland floor. Beetles and centipedes lie in wait, ready to jump out and chase their prey. The wolf spider lives up to its name!

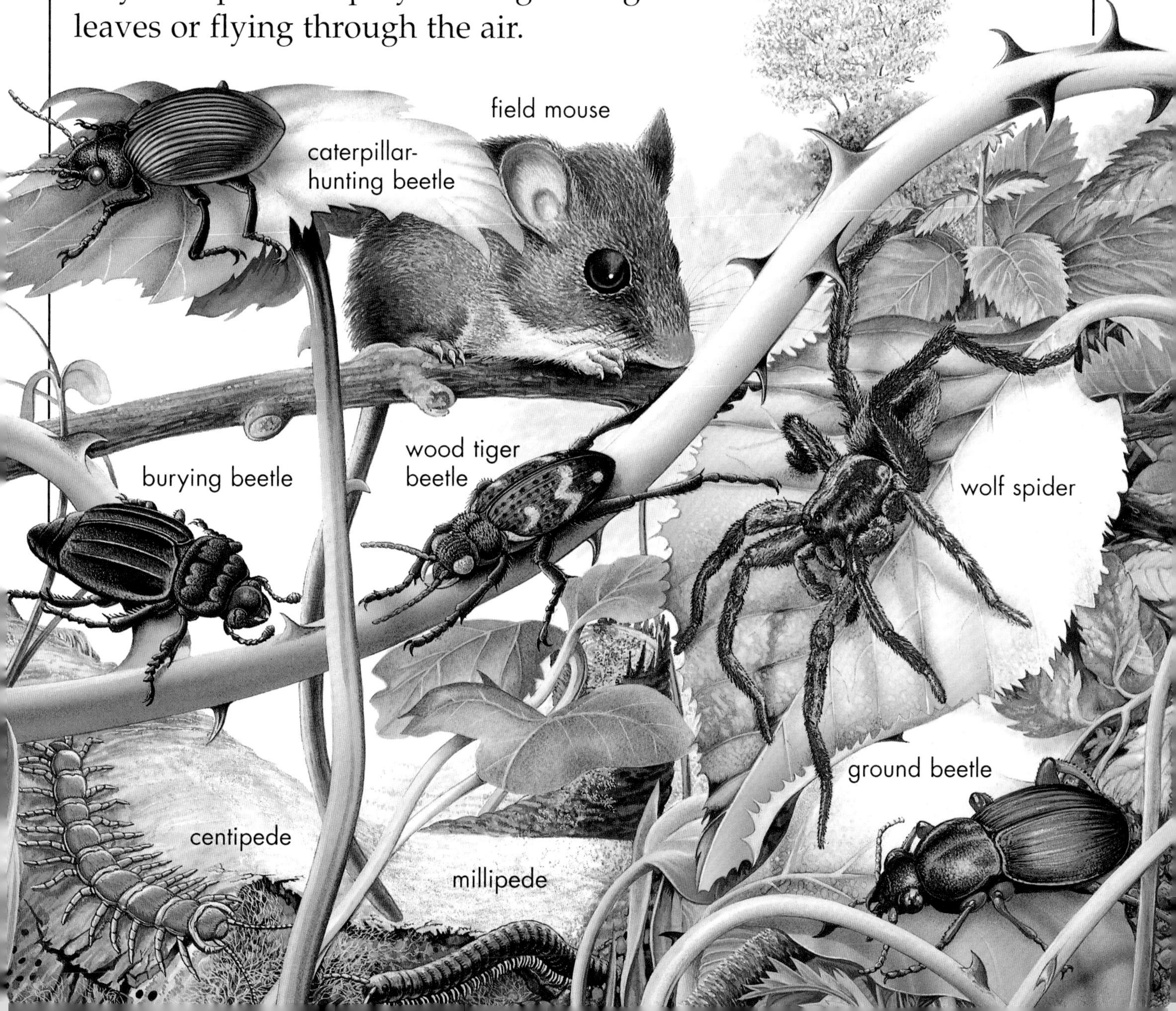

caterpillar-hunting beetle

field mouse

burying beetle

wood tiger beetle

wolf spider

centipede

millipede

ground beetle

Some carnivorous minibeasts set traps to catch their prey. Spiders spin webs with sticky threads to trap and hold flying insects. When an insect gets trapped, the spider bites it and injects a poison that paralyzes it. Then it wraps the insect in spider silk and injects it with enzymes that break down its body, turning it to a liquid the spider can suck up.

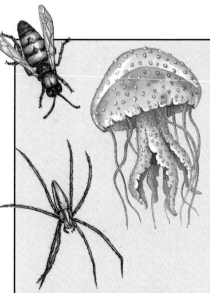

orb weaver spider

mesh-web spider

Poisonous Stings

Jellyfish, spiders, and hunting wasps kill their prey with a powerful sting. The wasps carry their prey to their nests to feed their larvae.

Spiders' Webs

Orb weaver spiders spin large webs to trap flying insects. Mesh-web spiders make webs to trap crawling insects. The nursery-web spider spins a netlike web over a plant to protect the eggs she has laid.

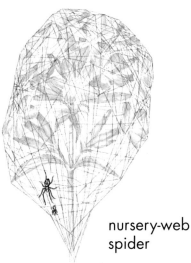

nursery-web spider

Do it yourself

At night, the woods come alive with minibeasts moving around in search of food. You can catch them in a pitfall trap—but make sure you return them to the woodland floor.

1. Find two plastic cups or other small containers and put one inside the other.

12

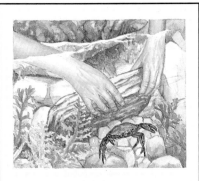

👁 Eye-Spy

Crabs are found on rocky shores, in tide pools, and under rocks. See how many you can find on the shore. You could try to entice them from their hiding places by dangling a small piece of meat on a piece of string.

Aerial Hunters

Dragonflies have large wings and enormous eyes that help them to hunt efficiently. They fly along stretches of water at speeds up to 29 miles per hour (48kph), looking for flying insects. Then they pluck their prey out of the air, using their spiky legs as a net.

2. Dig a hole and put both containers in it so that the top of the inside one is level with the ground.

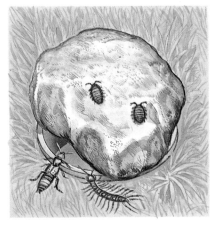

3. Put some meat or fruit in the container. Place a stone across the top, but do not cover it completely.

4. The next day, lift out the inside container. Now you can see what you have caught in the trap.

Runners, Leapers, and Creepers

Some minibeasts move across the ground very quickly, while others just crawl. Leaping insects can jump great distances. They have extra long hind legs that give them a powerful takeoff. The click beetle escapes from predators by lying on its back and playing dead. Then it suddenly jumps into the air, lands on its feet, and runs away. Worms do not have legs, but rely on muscles in their body to move them through the soil in a rippling motion. Snails glide along on their muscular foot.

Grasshoppers have muscular hind legs that are much longer than the other two pairs. These give the grasshopper a powerful push when it leaps. Once the grasshopper is in the air, it uses its wings to glide.

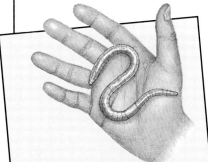

👁 Eye-Spy

A worm extends its body forward, then pulls the back part toward the front. See if you can feel the tiny bristles that help the worm to grip the ground as it moves.

Do it yourself

A garden snail moved 12 inches (31cm) in 2 min. and 13 sec. Beat this world record by racing your own snails.

1. You will need a board about 3 feet (1m) long and 20 inches (50cm) wide. Use string to divide the board into lanes. Hold the string tight with thumb tacks. Mark the start with chalk.

2. Place your snails at the start line and set them off!

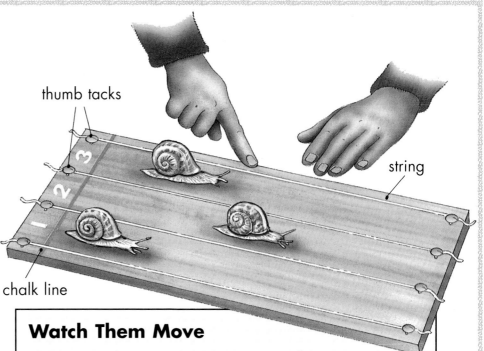

thumb tacks

string

chalk line

Watch Them Move

The best way to watch a snail or a slug move is to place it on a sheet of glass or clear plastic. Watch it from below, so that you can see the rippling movement of muscles in the foot of the animal. As it moves forward, it leaves behind a glistening trail of slime.

snail

slug

Looping Caterpillars

Some caterpillars move in a looping manner. They extend the front of their body forward and then pull up the back end to form a loop.

Flying Insects

Only birds, bats, and insects can fly. Wings allow these animals to travel great distances in search of food. Most flying insects have two pairs of thin, almost see-through wings, but some have just one pair. Beetles have two pairs, but the front pair is hardened to form a tough protective cover for the hind pair, which are folded out of sight. The ladybug has a pair of hard, red wings, and underneath are a pair of thin wings used for flight. The fastest fliers are dragonflies, horseflies, and hawkmoths, which can reach 35 miles per hour (58kph).

African giant swallowtail

Largest Wings

The world's biggest butterflies belong to the swallowtail family. The African giant swallowtail has a wingspan of about 9 inches (23cm).

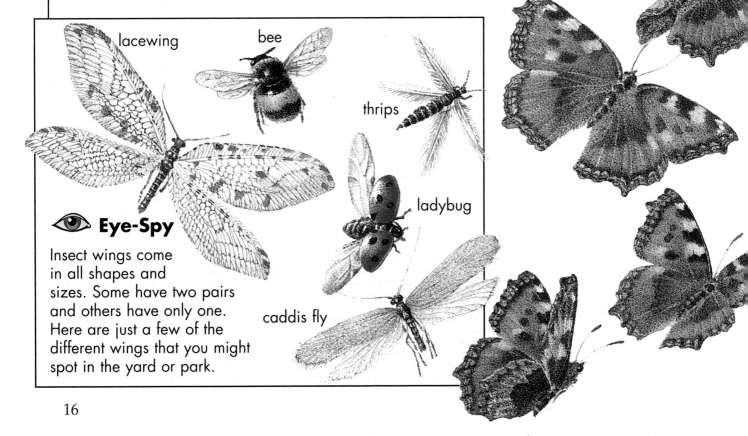

lacewing

bee

thrips

ladybug

👁 Eye-Spy

Insect wings come in all shapes and sizes. Some have two pairs and others have only one. Here are just a few of the different wings that you might spot in the yard or park.

caddis fly

Butterflies have a weak, fluttering flight. Their large wings beat slowly, up and down. The swallowtail butterfly has the slowest wing beat of any insect, just five wing beats per second.

Coming in to Land

This high-speed flash photograph of a bee shows how it holds out its wings to reduce speed before coming in to land on a leaf.

Do it yourself

Attract insects to your windowsill by planting flowers that are rich in nectar and have a strong scent.

1. Fill a window box with compost and water it well.

2. Sprinkle flower seeds onto the surface of the compost. Plant nasturtium seeds near the edge so that they trail over the sides as they grow. Others can be sprinkled in groups.

3. Cover the seeds with a thin layer of compost and wait for them to grow. Water whenever the soil looks dry.

Self Defense

All animals need to be able to defend themselves against predators. Beetles and wood lice have a heavy armor covering that is difficult to crush. Some insects stop their attackers by spraying them with acid or other chemicals. With clever camouflage, minibeasts can lie concealed and avoid being eaten. Their coloring may make them look like a piece of bark, a leaf, or part of a flower.

Warning Colors

The bright colors of the sea slug warn other animals that it is covered in sting cells and should not be eaten.

Eye-Spy

Many minibeasts are hard to spot in the yard because they are so well camouflaged. Caterpillars may be hidden among the leaves, camouflaged to look like bits of twig. Moths may have wings that are patterned to match the bark on which they rest. Snails may have shells that blend into their background. How many camouflaged minibeasts can you find in the yard or park?

rhinoceros beetle

Some minibeasts have tough outer skeletons. Others have claws or powerful legs. The silkworm caterpillar has dangerous, stinging bristles and the Io moth has eyespots to frighten off predators. The scorpion has a sting.

moth

silkworm
caterpillar

praying
mantis

illipede

scorpion

Do it yourself

Try this experiment to see how camouflage works.

1. Cut out a butterfly shape from a piece of black paper. Make a pattern of white dots on the butterfly and also on a large sheet of black paper.

2. Place the animal shape on the sheet of paper. Is it easy to spot? Put your finger on the shape and move it around. Is it easier to spot now?

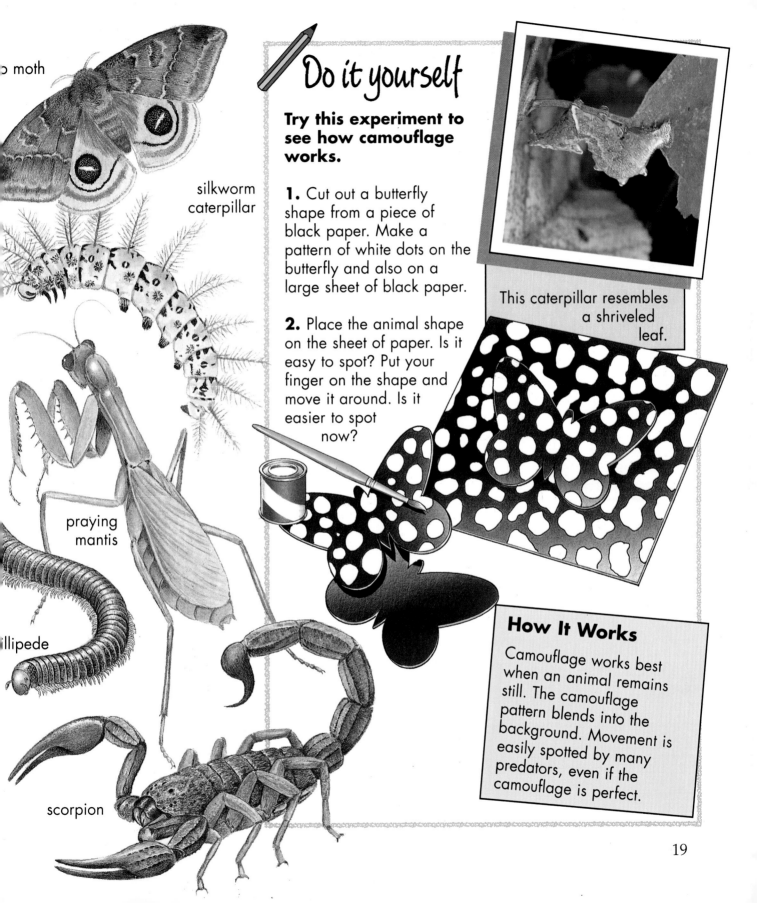

This caterpillar resembles a shriveled leaf.

How It Works

Camouflage works best when an animal remains still. The camouflage pattern blends into the background. Movement is easily spotted by many predators, even if the camouflage is perfect.

19

Friend or Foe?

Butterflies, bugs, and worms live everywhere, indoors and out. Most are harmless, but a few are pests. Slugs, Colorado potato beetles, and locusts damage crops. Crane fly larvae eat the roots of plants and slugs, snails, and caterpillars eat the leaves. Fortunately, there are just as many creatures that are useful. Hoverflies and ladybugs help in the garden by eating the aphids that feed on plants. Earthworm burrows aerate the soil and help water to drain away.

👁 **Eye-Spy**

How many different minibeast pests can you find in the yard?

honeybee

Garden soil is full of minibeasts. Crane fly and beetle larvae live underground until they grow into adult insects. Ants and worms dig tunnels and burrows. The worms and larvae are eaten by birds.

ladybug

aphids

butterfly

caterpillar

earthworm

crane fly larvae

ant

Colorado Potato Beetles

The yellow and black striped Colorado potato beetle is a major pest of the potato crop.

A swarm of locusts can devastate a huge area of crops in just a few hours, stripping the plants of all their leaves.

How It Works

Slugs need moisture, so they prefer places that are dark and damp. The traps create these conditions. The slugs may also try to eat the inside of the grapefruit skin.

Do it yourself

Try these slug traps in your garden.

1. Take half a grapefruit skin, a piece of wood, and some black plastic.

2. Place your traps near some vegetables on a warm, wet day when slugs will be active. Leave them overnight.

3. The next morning, see which trap was the most successful. Which of the three has the most slugs under it?

Honeybees

Bees make honey from the nectar they collect from flowers. Beehives are often put in orchards so that the flowers are pollinated by the bees as they look for nectar.

Silk Moths

Silk is made by the caterpillar of the silk moth. When they are ready to pupate, the caterpillars spin a cocoon of silk threads.

Ladybugs are welcome visitors to our gardens, because they feed on aphids.

How It Works

Worms like moisture, so they come out of their burrows when it rains. Vibrations trick the worms into thinking that it is raining, so they come to the surface.

Do it yourself

ants

woodworm holes

silver

Be a worm charmer.

1. Mark out an area of lawn 10 feet x 10 feet (3m x 3m).

2. Persuade the earthworms to come to the surface by playing music or prodding with a pitchfork.

Our homes are a source of food and warmth to many life-forms. Cockroaches eat almost anything, from crumbs of food to book covers. Microscopic dust mites, each smaller than a pinpoint, are everywhere. They especially like your bed, where there is a constant supply of dead skin cells. Bedbugs sometimes inhabit dirty beds, and tiny beetles live in carpets. Woodworm, the larva of a small beetle, attacks wood and leaves small holes. Clothes moths nibble holes in woolen clothes.

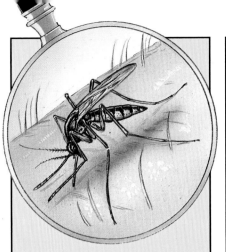

A mosquito pierces the skin and injects a substance that stops blood from clotting, so that it flows freely through the tiny puncture.

If you visit the kitchen at midnight, you may find some unwelcome visitors! Sugary foods attract ants, flies, and earwigs. Cockroaches and silverfish feed on crumbs. Lurking in the corners are spiders, waiting to catch their next meal.

flies

earwig

spider

cockroach

moth

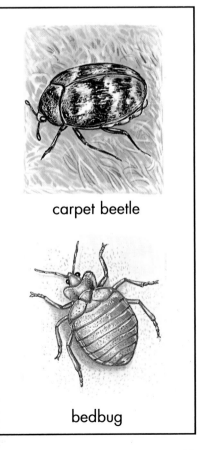

carpet beetle

bedbug

Life in the Water

A pool of water is quickly colonized by minibeasts. The first to arrive are the water beetles and mosquitoes, then other insects soon fly in. Ducks may bring the eggs of snails and fish on their feet. Soon the pool is brimming with life. Many microscopic animals swim in the water or live in the mud. In a pond, all the animals and plants live together as a community. The water lilies and other plants provide shelter and food for the plant eaters.

Water Spider

The water spider spins a balloonlike web that it fills with bubbles of air. It spends most of its time in the air-filled web and darts out to catch prey.

A wide variety of animal and plant life can be found in even the smallest pond. Pondweed and algae are food for plant eaters such as mussels and snails. The plant eaters are food for hunters such as back swimmers, water scorpions, and beetles.

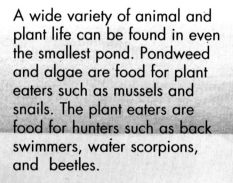

springtails

whirligig beetles

back swimmer

mosquito larvae

damselfly nymph

water mites

water scorpion

mayfly nymph

snail

back swimmer

leech

Water Beetles

Water beetles are often the first animals to arrive at a new pond. They spot pools of water from the air, by looking for reflections from the surface of the water. The great diving beetle may live for two years, feeding on insects, tadpoles, and small fish.

dragonfly

damselfly

Many minibeasts live on the surface of the water. Pond skaters and whirligig beetles skim across the surface, hunting for small insects.

frog

pond skater

snail

stickleback

Lily leaves provide shade, and dragonfly and damselfly nymphs use the iris leaves to climb out of the pond when it is time to change into adults.

great diving beetle

freshwater mussel

caddisfly larva

tadpoles

Do it yourself

The best way to find out about life in a pond is to go pond dipping.

1. You will need to take a net, a large bowl, some small containers, a magnifying glass, and your notebook. You may find a guidebook to pond life helpful.

2. Sweep the net through the water to catch the surface minibeasts. Empty the contents into the bowl and examine your catch.

3. You may need to move the animals into the containers to have a close look at them. Try to keep the plant eaters away from the meat eaters.

4. Use the magnifying glass to look at the smaller animals. Remember, you may have to count the number of legs to identify an animal.

5. More minibeasts may be found on the pondweed, under lily leaves, or on irises near the edge. Others can be found under stones.

6. Note down what you find. The types of minibeast are a good guide to how clean the water is.

7. Return all the animals to the water when you have finished.

Deep Water Warning

Water can be dangerous. Be very careful when working near it. Take an adult with you.

magnifying glass

containers

bowl

guidebook

notebook

net

Life under Logs and Stones

A pile of logs and dead leaves creates the damp and dark conditions that are ideal for animals such as wood lice and millipedes. These minibeasts play an important role in recycling the nutrients locked up in the remains of dead plants and animals. Beetles, millipedes, and wood lice break up leaves into tiny pieces. Other minibeasts eat the rotting wood. Then fungi and bacteria finish the process of decomposition.

Fallen leaves are broken up by small minibeasts and quickly rot. Among the leaves and logs are hunters such as centipedes and false scorpions. Frogs and toads may hunt here, too.

Centipede or Millipede?

A millipede has two pairs of legs on each segment, while a centipede has only one pair per segment.

toad

millipede

centipede

wood lice

worm

false scorpion

slug

springtail

Wood lice

Wood lice emerge at night to feed on dead leaves and wood. Their bodies are protected with a heavy armorlike covering. Some wood lice can roll up into a ball to protect their vulnerable body organs.

A Recycling Job

Many minibeasts act as garbage collectors, clearing up the remains of dead plants and animals. Flies gather around a dead mouse and lay their eggs on its body. Maggots hatch and feed on the rotting flesh. Soon, all that is left is a pile of bones.

Do it yourself

How many minibeasts can you find in a pile of leaf litter?

1. Collect leaf litter from the woods. Spread a large sheet of paper on a table and tip some leaf litter onto it. You will quickly spot the minibeasts moving around on the paper. Make sure the larger ones do not run off the edge.

2. Using a paintbrush and tweezers, put the minibeasts in little containers to examine them. Try not to mix plant eaters with meat eaters.

3. When you have finished, put all the animals back into the litter and return the litter to where you found it.

leaf litter

Do it yourself

Make mini-homes for animals in your yard or school grounds.

1. A clay flowerpot can make a bumblebee nest site. Put some wood chips or straw inside the pot. Then bury the pot upside down in a flower bed, with just the hole showing. Bumblebees may fly in through the hole and build a nest.

More Things to Try

If you have enough space, you could build a stone wall and earth bank. Stack the stones to form a double-sided wall with space in the center. Fill the middle with soil, making sure you leave lots of nooks and crannies. Plants will quickly cover the bank, while spiders, wood lice, and ants will hide between the stones.

2. Drinking straws can provide a home for small insects. Take a bundle of straws and block one end of each straw with mud. Then tie the straws together and hang them beneath a window ledge. Soon, small insects will creep into the straws.

3. Pile up logs and stones in a shady place in the yard. The moist and dark conditions will attract beetles, centipedes, and millipedes. Frogs and toads may spend the winter in the pile, too.

Living Together

Social insects live together in groups or colonies. Colonies form a community in which adults and young play a role. There is usually only one queen, and she is responsible for laying all the eggs. Most of the individuals are workers. Workers are female, and their jobs include building the home, finding food, keeping the home clean, and looking after the larvae. There are a few males to mate with the queen. Many bees and wasps live like this, and so do all ants and termites.

Weaver ants make nests by pulling several leaves together onto a branch and sticking them in place with a glue produced by the larvae.

A wild bees' nest contains more than 80,000 worker bees. There is a single queen bee and a few male drones. The nest is made up of wax combs suspended inside a hollow tree. Each comb contains hundreds of wax cells. The queen lays a single egg in each of the cells. The larvae hatch and are fed with pollen and honey by the workers. They then pupate to become new worker bees.

A termite colony may consist of several million termites. Together, they build a nest using mud glued with saliva. The nest reaches several yards above and below the ground. Hidden within the nest is a maze of tunnels, chambers for larvae, chambers for food and waste, and a complex system of ventilation shafts.

👁 Eye-Spy

In late summer, look for winged ants on patios and rock gardens. These are males and young queen ants that will fly away to start their own new colonies.

Soldier Termites

Soldier termites protect the colony. They attack enemies by injecting a poisonous chemical, or squirting a type of glue.

ventilation system

chamber

queen termite

tunnel

Index

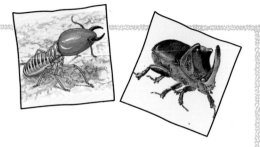

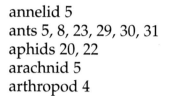